COCO GAUFF

BY LEIGH LEWIS

AMICUS LEARNING

Inspire is published by
Amicus Learning, an imprint of Amicus
P.O. Box 227
Mankato, MN 56002
www.amicuspublishing.us

Editor: Ana Brauer
Series Designer: Kathleen Petelinsek
Book Designer and Photo Researcher: Emily Dietz

Library of Congress Cataloging-in-Publication Data
Names: Lewis, Leigh, author.
Title: Coco Gauff / by Leigh Lewis.
Description: Mankato, MN : Amicus Learning, 2026. | Series: Inspire | Includes bibliographical references and index. | Audience: Ages 5-9 | Audience: Grades 2-3 | Summary: "Learn about American tennis star Coco Gauff and her accomplishments in an engaging profile packed with photos and fact-filled text suitable for young readers. Includes table of contents, glossary, further resources, and index"— Provided by publisher.
Identifiers: LCCN 2024044103 (print) | LCCN 2024044104 (ebook) | ISBN 9798892005173 (library binding) | ISBN 9798892005715 (paperback) | ISBN 9798892006255 (ebook)
Subjects: LCSH: Gauff, Coco, 2004—Juvenile literature. | Women tennis players—United States—Biography—Juvenile literature. | African American tennis players—Biography—Juvenile literature.
Classification: LCC GV994.G38 L48 2026 (print) | LCC GV994.G38 (ebook) | DDC 796.342092 [B]—dc23/eng/20241119
LC record available at https://lccn.loc.gov/2024044103
LC ebook record available at https://lccn.loc.gov/2024044104

Photo Credits: AP/Abaca Press/Sipa USA, cover, Corinne Dubreuil/Sipa USA, 6–7; Associated Press/Jean-Francois Badias, 19, Tim Ireland, 12–13; Getty Images/Clive Brunskill, 5, Frey/TPN, 9, Icon Sportswire, 18, Quality Sport Images, 14, Robert Prange, 20–21; Shutterstock/DeanHarty, 7, Leonard Zhukovsky, 16–17, lev radin, 10–11, M. Unal Ozmen, 16

Table of Contents

4 Tennis Star

7 On the Move

8 All in the Family

11 Aim Higher

12 Playing Her Idol

15 Cocomania

16 First Major Win

19 The Olympics

20 Helping Others

22 Super Stats

23 Glossary

24 Read More

24 On the Web

24 Index

Tennis Star

Coco Gauff steps up to the line. She tosses the ball high in the air. She serves fast and strong. The ball goes 128 miles per hour (206 kilometers per hour). **Ace**!

Gauff is an American professional tennis player.

Coco Gauff is a nickname. Her real name is Cori Gauff.

Gauff poses with her parents after the 2017 Junior US Open.

On the Move

Gauff's family lived in Atlanta, Georgia until she was seven. In 2011, her mom and dad quit their jobs to help her succeed in tennis. They moved so that Gauff could play year-round. Her home became Delray Beach, Florida.

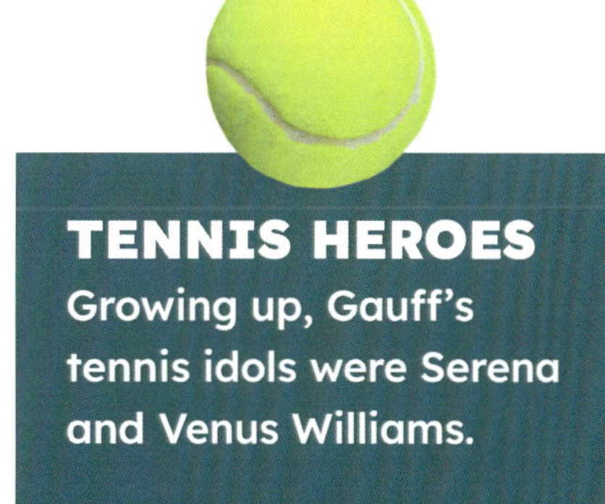

TENNIS HEROES
Growing up, Gauff's tennis idols were Serena and Venus Williams.

All in the Family

Gauff's mom became her homeschool teacher. Her dad became her coach. With their help, she went pro. She played her first pro match in 2018. She was 14. Her dad coached her until she was 16. As of September 2024, she is coached by Matt Daly and Jean-Christophe Faure.

Gauff's parents were athletes in college. They encouraged her to play tennis.

Gauff tells her fans to not give up on their dreams. Her motto is "dream big."

Aim Higher

Gauff knows her own playing style. She plays as **aggressive** as possible with a big serve. She's right-handed and uses a two-handed **backhand**. She encourages others to dream big and aim higher.

One of Gauff's dreams was to play Venus Williams. Her dream came true!

Playing Her Idol

Gauff played at Wimbledon in 2019. At 15, she was the youngest player ever to qualify. She got to play against Venus Williams in the first round. Gauff beat her! Gauff made it to the fourth round of the tournament that year.

Gauff quickly became a household name after beating Venus.

Cocomania

Beating Venus Williams made Gauff famous. She was a star on the Women's Tennis Association (WTA) tour. She was in magazines and TV shows. People recognized her in the streets. Everyone loves Coco Gauff!

First Major Win

Gauff won her first **Grand Slam** tournament in 2023. It was at the US Open. She beat Aryna Sabalenka. Gauff was the youngest American to win this tournament since Serena Williams in 1999.

Gauff kisses the trophy after winning the US Open.

EQUAL PAY

The US Open was the first sporting event to pay men and women equal prize money.

Gauff serves in the first round of the women's singles at the 2024 Paris Olympics.

The Olympics

In 2021, Gauff missed the Tokyo Olympics. She had Covid. At the 2024 Olympics, Gauff represented the US in Paris. She played singles, **doubles**, and **mixed doubles**. She didn't win a medal, but she is looking forward to the 2028 Olympics.

DOUBLES CHAMPION
Gauff played doubles with Kateřina Siniaková at the 2024 French Open. They won!

Helping Others

Gauff helps others. She plays charity matches. She donates money and tennis gear. She also helps renew city tennis courts. She's done this in both Atlanta and Delray Beach, her hometowns. Gauff inspires young athletes.

Gauff is an inspiration to kids around the world.

SPEAKING UP

In 2020, Gauff spoke at a Black Lives Matter rally. She encouraged others to use their voice.

new balance
FILA

SUPER STATS

CORI DIONNE GAUFF

Nickname: Coco

Birthday: March 13, 2004

Hometown: Delray Beach, Florida

AWARDS

Singles winner at US Open: 2023

Doubles winner at French Open: 2023

ACCOMPLISHMENTS

Ranked #2 in WTA singles: 2024

Ranked #1 in WTA doubles: 2023

Youngest player in 19 years to win a singles and a doubles Grand Slam title.

Only active women's tennis player to have her own signature sneaker.

GLOSSARY

ace A winning serve that the receiver does not touch.

aggressive Making an all-out effort to win or succeed.

backhand A tennis stroke that involves a forward movement of the arm with the back of the hand facing outward.

doubles Two people playing tennis against two others.

Grand Slam The four most important tournaments in tennis: the French Open, the US Open, the Australian Open, and Wimbledon.

mixed doubles A tennis team of one man and one woman.

READ MORE

Abdo, Kenny. **Coco Gauff.** Abdo Zoom, 2021.

Dittmer, Lori. **Tennis.** Creative Education, 2020.

Laughlin, Kara L. **Tennis.** The Child's World, 2024.

ON THE WEB

Biography: Coco Gauff
https://www.biography.com/athlete/coco-gauff

Olympics: Coco Gauff
https://olympics.com/en/athletes/coco-gauff

INDEX

Delray Beach, Florida, 7, 20
doubles, 19
family, 6–7, 8, 9
French Open, 19
Olympics, 18–19
Sabalenka, Aryna, 16
US Open, 16
Williams, Serena, 7, 16
Williams, Venus, 7, 12–13, 14, 15
Wimbledon, 13
Women's Tennis Association (WTA), 15

About the Author

Leigh Lewis is a children's author who loves her three kids, traveling, pickleball, and telling stories. She has lived in the US, Russia, Japan, England, Greece, and Turkey. Check out her books at leighlewisbooks.com.